Big Woods Bird

An Ivory-bill Story

Written by Terri Roberts Luneau
Illustrated by Trevor Bennett

For all the little children:
Amanda, Annie, Charlie, Evan, & Cole

Special thanks to Rhonda, Allison, and Foster

Published by Kury Lane Inc., Little Rock, Arkansas ♦ kurylane@swbell.net ♦ Copyright 2005, All Rights Reserved
No portion of this book may be reproduced without the express written consent of the publisher.
No animals were harmed in the making of this book. Not responsible for injuries resulting from misuse of this book.
ISBN 0-9768839-0-2 ♦ Library of Congress Control Number: 2005903949 ♦ 1st edition, 1st printing

Kury Lane Inc.

Old tall trees in a lake so still,

Branches on the water and I think I will

Paddle my canoe among the mallards and the fishes.

Watch out for snakes! Listen for their hisses!

Life is lively in the Big Woods deep

Where the tall buck romps and the doe will sleep

Upon soft moist soil beside quiet waters

Raising wildlife sons and wildlife daughters.

Thrashers thrash and warblers warble.

But I'm listening and looking for something special

That's a flash of white with a crest of red

Upon the back of a mighty black head.

Big Woods bird, I know you're here.

Big Woods magic, don't you disappear!

You hide in the thickets and the treetops too.

I watch and I wait 'cause I want to find you.

Sliding through the tree trunks, alone I float

Watching water-walkers walk beside my boat.

They scoot along the water then stop and stand

Just like the other bugs can do on dry land!

Tree tops creak and groan and sway

Waving thin branches as if to say

"Hello" to the chimney swifts flying on high

Or "Good Day" to the butterflies fluttering by.

Coming out of the shadows, pushed by the wind,

I startle a heron as I round the bend.

With such tall skinny legs it's hard to walk,

So he gives up and flies away with a squawk.

Big Woods bird, I know you're here.

Big Woods magic, don't you disappear!

I read lots of books and I studied your picture,

Ready at last for this great wild adventure.

Western storms rise, they billow and grumble.

Eastward they travel with thunders that rumble

And scare little bunnies into holes in the ground

While spiders hold tight as their webs wave around.

Winds weave their way through the Tupelo branches.

Cypress knees watch turtles taking their chances

Jumping off logs and making small splashes

As rain falls hard and lightning flashes.

I pull down my hat to cover my head

And wonder if you have a safe dry bed

For you and your mate and maybe a baby

In the hollowed out hole in the tree far above me.

Big Woods bird, I know you're here.

Big Woods magic, don't you disappear!

For there was a time when you were king

Of the Big Woods tall and your call would ring.

All that you needed was room to fly,

Trunks to pound, and open sky.

Ba-bam! Ba-bam! As you chisel away,

Hunting for grub worms for dinner each day.

Gray clouds lighten, brighten, and thin.

Otters swim in and out of their den

In the moss covered log under the trees

As sundrops sparkle on shiny clean leaves.

Out in the distance I hear, "Kent! Kent!"

I see something fly! Can't tell where it went!

Feathers of white flew swiftly away!

Was it an Ivory-bill? I can't really say!

Big Woods bird, I know you're here.

Big Woods magic, don't you disappear!

I watch and I wonder, I hope and I pray

That it really was you I spotted today.

Sun-up was early, sundown comes soon

For me and the birds and the masked raccoon,

Who wanders my way to be introduced

By the old barred owl that hoots from his roost.

With maps in my backpack and camera in hand

I'll come back tomorrow to explore this great land.

By canoe or on foot, alone or with others.

Hoping there's an Ivory-bill for me to discover.

So long you have hidden and many would think

That your time has passed and you are extinct.

But I search because I believe you're alive —

A mighty woodpecker that learned to survive!

The Rediscovery of the Ivory-billed Woodpecker

The Ivory-billed Woodpecker, the largest woodpecker ever to live in North America, has been considered extinct since the middle of the 20th Century. However, on February 11, 2004, Mr. Gene Sparling spotted what he thought might be an Ivory-bill while he was kayaking in the Big Woods swamp in eastern Arkansas.

He was excited about his sighting and contacted a birding expert at the Cornell Laboratory of Ornithology. Soon a team of individuals, which included local birding experts, university professors, conservationists, and woodpecker experts, was formed. This team became known as the Big Woods Conservation Partnership.

Their goal was to prove that the Ivory-bill still lived, and that it was living in eastern Arkansas. Photographic evidence would be necessary to convince the world that the bird was not extinct.

Ivory-bills nest in holes in tall trees. They feed on grubs found in dying trees, as well as on nuts and fruit. And they need lots of room to roam. Scientists believe that each pair of Ivory-bills needs many square miles of old forest. Unfortunately, most of the original forest in the United States was cut down. There are now areas where the forest is growing old again, making good habitat for Ivory-bills. However, these areas are generally remote, and only hunters, fishermen, and a few avid nature-lovers, like Mr. Sparling, visit there often.

Searchers, like David Luneau, spent many hours in the Big Woods looking for the Ivory-billed Woodpecker. Canoes with electric trolling motors, video cameras, and binoculars were some of the tools used in the search. Camouflaged clothing was worn because bright colors scare wildlife away.

Searching for an Ivory-bill involves spending long hours in the woods. The searchers used canoes painted with colors that would blend into the swamp. They sat quietly for hours watching the woodlands, watching the skies, and hoping that an Ivory-bill would fly over. They used binoculars to help them see. Some carried video cameras. Others set up motion-detecting still cameras hoping to snap a photograph of an Ivory-bill. Still others set up remote recording devices that were designed to listen for Ivory-bills. A tall "cherry-picker" was brought to the area. This machine lifted watchers up to the top of the tallest trees so they could look across the tree tops and down into the swamp. All hoped to prove that the Ivory-bill was there.

Several more sightings were reported in the late winter and early spring. In April 2004 a video was taken of a large black and white bird flying away from the canoe of two of the searchers. Researchers were able to study this video and determine that it really was the Ivory-billed Woodpecker!

This was great news for bird lovers, and now there is a renewed hope that this wonderful woodpecker may continue to live in the southern Big Woods.

Conservationists soon began working to find ways to preserve the remaining forests and to expand them where possible. Maybe one day, there will again be plenty of room for Ivory-bills.

Some of the trees are hundreds of years old and have grown very large. It would take three people to reach around the bottom of this cypress. Beautiful moss and ferns thrive on the tree trunks near the water.

About the Story

Big Woods Bird was written because the author was a first hand witness of the extraordinary search that was conducted during 2004 and 2005 in the Big Woods of Arkansas. She was able to accompany her husband David on several trips into the swamp and learn first hand about the wildlife and natural beauty of the area. Watching the team of searchers and listening to the stories they told of the sightings inspired her to want to share that interest and love with others and to help instill that love and wonder in children.

About the Author

Terri Roberts Luneau is a Certified Public Accountant who enjoys both birds and children's books. She lives in Little Rock, Arkansas, with her husband David. They have two children, Andrea and Kevin.

About the Artist

Trevor Bennett is a Studio Art major at the University of Arkansas at Little Rock and a personal friend of the Luneau family. He is also an Eagle Scout and a musician. He graduated from Parkview High School in Little Rock, where he and his family live.

Tall Cypress and Water Tupelo trees are the most common trees found in the Big Woods swamp. There are many beautiful sights to see, amazing animals to enjoy, and a lot to learn if you ever get a chance to canoe the Big Woods of Arkansas.